BUDDHA IN THE GARDEN

BUDDHA IN THE GARDEN

poems

Cathie Desjardins

Tasora Press/Itasca
5120 Cedar Lake Road
Minneapolis Minnesota 55416

Cover design by Tristan Spence

ISBN 978-1-934690-72-7

Manufactured in the United States of America

For David—

*Heavy lifter, fence-mender,
helpmeet, sweetheart*

TABLE OF CONTENTS

Before / 3

AUTUMN

Weather Report / 7

Ask Me / 8

October (Homage to Emily Dickinson) / 9

The Moon and The Melon / 10

Cutting Onions / 11

Fall in the Community Garden / 12

Welcome Poem / 13

November / 14

WINTER

Spy Pond in Winter / 17

Some Ways of Looking At Snow / 19

Faulty / 20

One Day in March / 21

as if hydrangeas / 22

Bitter / 23

Amaryllis / 24

Winter Haiku / 25

WHAT THEY SAY

Alstroemeria / 29

Bonsai Hinoki Cypress / 30

Violas in a Pot / 31

Crocuses / 32

GRANDES DAMES

One Summer Her Job / 35

Plaint / 36

What She Wore / 38

Boxed In / 39

The Creation of the Birds / 41

After the World War / 43

SPRING
Failed Invocation to the Muse / 47

That Blue / 49

Because the Sparrows / 50

Spring Snippings / 52

Outsider / 53

Acolyte of Green / 55

Hellebore / 56

Pea-planting Ceremony / 58

Bird Talk / 59

City Bulbs / 60

Squirrely / 61

Pasqueflower / 62

The Uses of Things / 63
SUMMER
You Ask / 67

Buddha in the Garden / 69

The Last Thing / 71

As We Go / 72

The First Tiny Buddha / 73

The Second Tiny Buddha / 74

Verge / 76

Raspberry Instructions / 77

Field Day at Spy Pond / 79

Flora / 81

Pink Hibiscus / 82

Provincetown / 83

What Happens / 84

Summer Snippings / 85

Stanley's Garden / 86

Paradise is made of grunt labor and a love for the garden far too old to bargain with, tame, or understand.

—Wendy Johnson

A garden is always a series of losses set against a few triumphs, like life itself...There the door is always open into the "holy"—growth, birth, death.

—May Sarton

BEFORE

Late fifties, we left the southside of Pittsburgh, our
asphalt-shingled half a slanting duplex,
moved to the South Hills where they'd scooped
out a hole for our ranch house.

Where did that yellow-brown dirt go? We had
a drop-off so steep my mother followed a dump truck
to where it was ditching fill, asked them to bring it
to our house so we'd have a yard behind the cinderblock
garage where my father, improvising taxidermy,
nailed eyeless fish heads with razor teeth
onto boards: walleye, pike.

The dumped fill sank to lumpy platforms. Along
one edge my parents planted poplars a foot
apart, sawed them to stumps
when they tangled sewer lines.
My Aunt Lavinia gave us a stick in a jug that grew
to a willow tree where the ground
plunged down to woods.

People dumped trash at a cut
along the sidewalk but no one went down
among the sunken trees scanted of light.
Spiky burrs would cling from plants tall as me,
space pods, I thought, though by then
Captain Video was gone from TV.

When I was nine I got poison ivy in winter
carrying carrots over the snow for bunnies
I hadn't seen, nor did I think to look for tracks.

I remember vines hanging from the trees
the way they did in Tarzan movies
and the smell of damp ground,
though I never saw a *crick*, what we called creeks.

Now I want to overlay a transparency, say *burdock*
for the space pods, *wild grapevines*, or maybe
oriental bittersweet for the rough vines thick
as my wrist. I don't remember my breathcloud
in the cold, my tread over hardening ground.
I had no names for what grew, no way to know
if it was ugly or beautiful.

AUTUMN

WEATHER REPORT

The solo jazz piano on the car radio
is saying it will continue to rain
in big liquid drops, slowing
at times until it almost
stops, but periodically becoming a drizzle
of tiny urgent needles.

Then, some partial clearing, followed
by a steady downbeat of notes and plops—

interludes of sun and clouds
will continue
for the rest of our natural lives.

ASK ME

Ask me what it means, this time of year,
this time between, when growth slows
and tomatoes hang milky green on the vines—
when any night might bring a blackening frost

to twist the flowers on their stems—
when trees reveal their deeper nature,
blazing scarlet, paling to gold,
or fiercely gripping green till it curls brown.

Ask me what it means, this time of currents,
warm and cold, and I will say:
I know it for my own time, my skin growing
papery as leaves, ridged with veins.

I don't know which tree I'll be
slipping toward a colder, darker time—
brazen, or wan, or loosening my sheaves
in a heap to stand bare and elemental.

It's what sends me out in early dusk,
to gather with cold fingers
snapdragon, pansy, aster, rose,
a last small bouquet.

OCTOBER

Homage to Emily Dickinson

Golden slabs of light are laid
Across pale afternoons—
Above the dusk, leaves snag late light
Where tinsel airplanes zoom—

Unkempt, the fading garden sprawls
Before the frost forgives—
Quick birds will gather up the chaff
Of all that's left—unsieved

Outdoors where we have worked and played
As if in spacious rooms—
Only fit for forays now—
Before cold drives us in—

Stage left or right the birds perform
As extras in the drama—
In fleets they swirl, advance, depart
Configured for the warmer—

Above, the sky withdraws and pales
Indifferent to our lives—
Perhaps it's we desert the field
To move apart—inside

Basil pales, but—crushed—sends up
Lost smell of sun on fingers—
Seed beads are strung along thin stems—
Austere décor that lingers—

The verdant stops—what's green won't thrive--
So scanted by the sun—
When someone speaks too soon— held breath
Then rain beats all to ground

9

THE MOON AND THE MELON
scroll by Zhu Da, 1689

Squat melon mounding to a belly-button stem
seems to be communing
with the low moon, each orb
a single brush stroke,
sure sweep shunning flourish:
The mind relaxes,
vegetative harmony...

But the bronze plaque tells another tale:
Zhu Da's family died under the sword
of a new dynasty and he wandered
the world, drawing, writing

No uprising...has a hope of success.
The moon so round when the melons rise
Everyone points to the moon cakes,
But hope that the melons will ripen
is a fool's dream.

Zhu Da, forgive me for finding abundance
where you meant emptiness. I wanted
the comic comfort of the lopsided melon facing
the fat, rising moon: an elegant doodle,
not a drama.

CUTTING ONIONS

I take no precautions against weeping.
Slicing into the firm flesh,
I think of those wavy lines in comic books
that rise from a reek.

Nose-tickle zing distracts
from the creamy opaque tones
painters choose for nudes.
I hear my art history teacher

droning about "painterly qualities."
Thump of the cleaver
as I cry soundlessly,
Hah! I think: such easy tears

compared to those
from life's telenovela dramas,
those black tides roaring
towards us, underground.

FALL IN THE COMMUNITY GARDEN

Gate's clang flushes them from their economies:
upside-down chickadees harvesting sunflower umbrels,
white tipped juncos, song sparrows foraging final kernels,
a startle of small birds gathering seeds.

Contests are done: whether morning glories will strangle
squash, green pumpkins ever glow orange.
Abandoned to weeds, what's left to forage?
A few perfect raspberries dangle,

But touched, turn mush from a bleeding core.
Broken stems of sunflowers circle in air
creaking in stiff loops. No one's here
as if the end of summer had closed a door.
Keeled cosmos tilt crazily in slant light—
whatever's akimbo will never be set straight.

WELCOME POEM

i think
    you are the tide
and i
    the ragged grass
beside the sea
    singing
a thin song
    waiting to be
drawn under

NOVEMBER

Three days of rain
and the garden begins
to be ruined.

Mornings so clouded
it seems already
the early dark.

Dahlia stems snapped:
petal mops the size
of human heads dangle.

Berries, peppers
spot and rot, sag
closer to earth.

Watering can in the rain—
foolish as always
I thought to need it again.

WINTER

SPY POND IN WINTER

It's like the dream where you open
                         a closet or find stairs
to a whole new part
                         of your house—

Land of Ice, village
                         of people sliding, icefishing,
veering around
                         exuberant as if
they're on a
                         whole new planet.

Sharp wind gusting
                         loose snow
could almost make
                         an ice mirage:
bygone skaters in woolen
                         caps, handknitted scarves,
whizzing past without
                         a thought of growing up,
 growing old,
                         crews of men
and thick horses hauling
                         squat crystal blocks on sleds
to ice houses on the shore
                         to be packed in sawdust
and shipped to the tropics.

Over at the playground,
rungs of the blue structure
                    our son climbed
decades ago
                    are crusted white,
crayon color dumptrucks
                    stalled in snow—
no cleared swaths.
                    I pry the red levers of the scoop
loose, swoop up snow,
                    plop it in a different spot.

Some kids turn up, blocky
                    as packages in snowsuits,
frolic a little.
                    I want to warn their
hovering parents:
                    You think this will go on
but soon they'll be taller
                    than you, then gone.
The frozen world makes it seem eternal
                    but the seeds of next summer's asters
are already strewn under the snow.

                    But the wind roughens
and the kids are shrieking now,
                    skidding on their backs
down the rollers
                    of the bumpy slide.

SOME WAYS OF LOOKING AT SNOW

I

Winter vaporizing
leaves wet shadows
on the sidewalk

II

Heavy metal foot dragging in the night--
snowplow sparkscraper invades our dreams

III

Children on the corner
are carving shelves in the snowbanks
the size of their curled bodies

IV

Icicles bar the windows
The snow has begun to take prisoners

V

Breathe in white, breathe out blue:
the snow and its shadows

VI

Snow is so deep
rabbits leave prints of their bodies
like dinosaur footprints

VI

Sharp wind scrubs us over
washboard ice

VII

In the dark, mounded snow
waits like a patient animal

VIII

Nearly spring:
deep in the forest,
white birches camouflage
snow abiding

FAULTY

Rusted nearly through at the base
of their pale green throats,
the amaryllis buds are trying to bloom,
like a person with a tracheotomy

trying to say a poem. Buds leak
dark red when I snip them
from their weakened stalks, trimming
them to clean pale stubs to put in water.

Day to day, the largest furled bud
is loosening into white wrapped wings,
the other three buds each a smaller
version like Russian nesting dolls

plumping into white petals
veined green, but their nubs
are softening underwater and I don't know
if they can ripen without earth.

Lying next to you on a sleety day
I look over at them wondering
if I should furl my body closed
now that it's faulty, diagnosed,

or whether I should open
deeper and deeper to you in case
this is the last
of intimacy we will know.

ONE DAY IN MARCH

the sun comes out.
I ferry the last two
scraggly basil plants
around the room
from patch
to patch of sun,

collect rigid pouches
of teabags and coffee filters,
squid of banana peels,
dayglo orange rinds,
drag the bucket outside
to the mound
of thawing compost.

Ruckus of birds
advertising for mates;
I prop up the lid
of the coldframe,
sprinkle in lettuce seeds
light as chopped thread,
scrape the tines
of the garden fork across
the blank paper
of stiff dirt.

Now I can
chop
the last
three
small
potatoes
I dug
last Fall,
add them
to soup.

as if hydrangeas

could mend a heart: even indigo hydrangeas,
creamy centers spumed green---
blue hydrangeas, bought in winter, carried,
paperwrapped into the cold, a thing to carry
besides useless sorrow for my daughter
whose first sweetheart has become her first heartbreak

a thousand paper petals won't whisper comfort
when trust has rusted through to grief

I want to feed her oranges,
to brush out her long hair;
to pay her a lifetime allowance
never to be sad

Instead I give her these, hydrangeas bruised
so blue they are nearly purple--
as if hydrangeas
could mend a heart

BITTER

late winter, New England

Because the world
was frozen,
my brain wove cobweb
artifices, replaying
he said she said she said
to blame and decide
who was most
foolish.

I ate rice from a pot
burnt on the bottom, rice
almost too scorched
to taste.

I yanked on strands
of the same wet knots
and my hair
turned gray. Outside
the wind
was worrying,
worrying all the
edges.

Sun a decal in the sky.
The only thing left
to stumble outside
and kneel, blinded
on damp ground
trying to remember,
keening over and over
Nothing can stop green.

AMARYLLIS

Like a horror movie,
flicking the grimy light switch,
picking my way down the ancient
steep stairs to the basement.

Woosh of the furnace,
high cobwebs in corners.
Under the folding table,
smell of musty earth.

I bend to speak to them
in a low voice, scaly bulbs
in huddled pots with papery swords
of dead leaves.

Some have sent out limp eel-
pale leaves from their stumps
like hair or nails
growing from corpses.

It's up to you, I tell them
But I want you to know
there's a warmer place upstairs.
If I stealth-boost

the thermostat, even warmer.
Show me a fleck of green,
and I'll bring you there,
to warm water, sun.

Silence from them,
swaddled in flaking onion skin.
But I'll be back.
I've seen Resurrection.

WINTER HAIKU

CRUNCH
On a warming day
feet stomp lingering ice:
revenge for winter

In a vase
four-day-old tulips, crumpled silk ballgown
fading, shiny, pink

Moon at dusk:
silver shell in the ocean
of wavy blue sky

UNDERPANTS
Laundry on the porch
celebrating winter's end
flaps a wild line dance

WHAT THEY SAY

ALSTROEMERIA

Peruvian Lily; Lily of the Incas; Parrot Lily

We are a tame wilderness,
leopard-stippled pastels,
like Rousseau's jungles
modeled on the Sunday jardins.
Like his nudes, we always
look arranged.

You will find us
in any season,
murmuring each to each.
We fade so slowly
you might think we
are only lightening in color
with a certain shiny brittleness.

Bred for florists,
we deny our birth in dirt,
gracing tables
like intelligent girls
wanting only
to be thought pretty.

BONSAI HINOKI CYPRESS
Chaemaecypris obtusa

More times than I have twigs
this has happened:
the sun, gone so long
behind the low hills, mounts
the roof slats and the walking
trees come, barkless and pale,
to hover near us with uneasy
motions.

The tiny maples, the
azaleas, offer their flowering
buds, but I provide only
this constant green.
I've thickened into an
endurance that disregards
seasons. Even now, as the sun
mounts, no one knows if,
after centuries, any
thread
of sap still
rises in me.

VIOLAS IN A POT

Choose us, choose us!
Cousins linked
by a kin of colors:
purple velvet,
lavender pale as scent bottles,
buttery white promising
happiness.

Like long-suffering parents,
the more we give,
the sturdier we grow,
as if we'd always known
our blooming
was destined for others.

CROCUSES

Crocus vernus

The brick convenience store wall
by the parking lot

has trapped the sun
and unfurled our silk:

Who can predict the uses
of commerce?

GRANDES DAMES

ONE SUMMER HER JOB

for Katherine Swift, gardener and garden writer

was to write words
to embellish catalogues
for David Austin roses,
enticing souls shriveled
as overstored potatoes
in winter.

She'd visit the roses
at his Shropshire nursery
with a photographer
and a retired perfumier
who pronounced on their fragrance—
coffee? curry? ripe pear?

Each day they got their list
of roses coming in to flower.
But—how to say how
Duchesse de Montebello
differed from *Duchesse d'Angouleme?*

She taught herself: *leaf, sepal, thorn,*
semi-double, cupped,
rosette, in truss or spray,
streaked or veined...

But among the carnival opulence,
how to say even the white
she loved best? — ivory,
paper white, cream silk,
brimful of yellow stamens,
coconut ice, shadowed lilac,
shaded apple-green:

Writing for me became a way of seeing.

PLAINT

> *The more I read, the more I am convinced that I should have lived in*
> *an age when seriousness and noble thoughts found an echo.*
>   Vita Sackville-West 1892-1962

Sundays they know not to come to the Tower
where I'm tethered till the wretched column,
the garden feature for the local paper, is done.
Fifteen guineas a week for fifteen years.

The blue glass from Turkey above me on the shelf—
if only it were a sea to bear me away.
Turning Sissinghurst from a rubbish heap
to a garden was easier than this.

Why don't the villagers know
how to keep anemones happy
or see for themselves how dark shrubs
for backdrop make flowers explode with light?

What of art, history, letters? —Merit
in the ways I've learned to wheel
characters in novels like constellations,
and turn a sonnet deftly, like a ship
at the eighth line, moor it to the mainland?

When I performed my dramas
for the servants and mama's gentlemen callers,
they'd clap until their hands stung.
Now my calf-bound volumes earn
only the blandest mention in The Times.

The talk is all about awkward Tom Eliot
come from America with his false English accent
and dunghill despair, and that Irishman James Joyce.
Virginia says his writing is like
an adolescent scratching pimples.
Why won't they call me a Woman of Letters?

36

Now I'm famous for scribbling about violets
and then they troop here by the busload
to see how it's done. I've never minded
getting my hands dirty, but these garden columns,
this penny postcard work—
grubbing of the worst sort.

WHAT SHE WORE
(for Vita Sackville-West 1892-1962)

A farm girl's uniform of trousers and gaiters
had no place in the drawing room,
the society ladies said, disapproving
of her riding breeches and lace-up boots,
custom-made in London with a slip pocket
for secateurs, pruning shears ever at the ready.

Silk blouses, a man's jacket, dangling earrings and
ancestral pearls: for decades she wore them
in all weathers, in her gorgeous youth and when,
as Virginia confided in her diary, Vita ran to fat,
high-color lips and cheeks gone blotchy.

Once her mother, demented or ill,
demanded back the dozen extra pearls
she'd gifted her daughter. Out in the street,
to her chauffeur's consternation,
Vita ripped them from her knotted string,
nearly spilling them in the gutter.

Did she find the shortened string
more tidy while seeding and snipping?
But encumbrances were a specialty:
a dozen female lovers she never
abandoned, husband and sons to whom
she always returned, dogs and books
and tapestries, jewels, ancestral loot.

Even Sissinghurst, *a dump of a place*
they'd bought for £15,000—
300 acres of abandoned rubbish, a clogged moat,
she turned into the most famous garden in England,
digging, pruning, in cord trousers and pearls.

BOXED IN
(Celia Thaxter 1835-94)

Toads in a box brought from the mainland by boat
part of your vendetta against *the awful slugs*.
Only three dusty hummocks poking up until
the garden hose splashed dirt to mud and five,

nine, dozens hopped, chirred toadsongs in hose rain.
All gone now, like the songbirds. Only seagulls roost, coast.
Celia, on the Appledore Ferry I thought of your crossings,
balancing trays of golden poppies in eggshells

to plant out on the island in spring: *The shell
can be broken from the oval ball of roots
without disturbing them and they are
transplanted almost without knowing it.*

I hoped to learn from you what to do
so a garden could flutter in a seaside dance.
*Plants are conscious of love
and respond to it as they do to nothing else.*

*A lonely child, living on a lighthouse island…
every blade of grass, every humblest weed
was precious in my sight and I began a little garden
when not more than five years old.*

Grown, you arranged flowers by height
each day at your family's grand hotel in the room
the grand piano made into a salon. Whittier,
Hawthorne, Emerson came. Childe Hassam

painted you, whitehaired in a white dress, windblown,
signature rose at your bosom. I look for your underpinning
corset, guessing how tightly you were bound, caretaker
of invalid husband, parents, brain-damaged son.

I trekked to discover your island garden
was a rectangle, thirty by fifty feet:
no spans, no arches, curves, no potager—only a fence
to keep off the wind from a box of floral bonbons.

I'd hoped for artful vistas, frames
to see anew, but flowers were enough
for you: *mostly old-fashioned…the strongest growers,
the freest bloomers, the most beautiful of their kind.*

Your cottage is burned down now with its fairytale tangle,
a piazza you *draped with Honeysuckles, blue and white Clematis,
Cinnamon Vine, Wistaria, Nasturtiums, Morning Glories,
Japanese Hops, Woodbine and Wild Cucumber.*

Your strong fingers sawed windows
through that thicket, carved leafy boxes
for guests to track pale sails on clear nights,
watch the moon fling glitter on the waves.

THE CREATION OF THE BIRDS

painting by Remedios Varo (1908-1963)

Are you woman turning owl, or owl turning woman?—
you with feathered torso, human feet still
on the stone floor, downcast owl eyes of a bird.
Was it you who made this odd instrument,
egg-shaped apparatus? transforming
what enters through oval windows in the room—

stardust? night air? —imported to the dusky room
through glass tubes you might have blown, owl-woman.
They stretch to a palette, where their ether is transformed
to red, blue, yellow. What's distilled
is what you paint with, stylus linked to a stringed instrument
over your heart. You deftly draw a bird

already flitting from you, escaping with other birds
through the arched windows of the room.
Sketching them to life, you are the instrument,
doing *opus mulierum*, the work of women—
alchemy—as you transform what's still
to quick flight, as you transform

this space to a dream laboratory, transformed
yourself to embody when women were birds,
those who made *cucurbit, alembic, retort, still*—
devices of incubation and change, leaving room
for things emerging beyond what a woman
imagined, no matter how clever her instruments.

The insouciant birds don't care about instruments.
They've become themselves, no urge to transform.
To beget them took an owl-woman
who knows the predilections of birds,
borrowing nature's secrets but making room
for colors and the ghost of music, a still-

ness deeper than anyone had yet fathomed as still.
Here in this arena of mystery instruments,
a gusseted box, a triangle prism, serve the room's
alchemies. Amphorae switch arcs of water, transforming
water to water, same to same, as owl women draw birds,
as a female painter might imagine an owl-woman.

Remedios Varo, artist, woman, whose secrets taught you to be so still?
To paint the flighty birds, shape these occult instruments?
What transformed you to architect of this mystic room?

AFTER THE WORLD WAR

Gertrude Jekyll 1843-1932
Edwin Luytens 1869-1944

I

Bumps he called her. He, an architect of 19,
she, 46, already famous. Her failing vision
made her reinvent the formal English garden,
cultivating color as pure form, daylight its brush, seeking
graduating harmonies culminating into gorgeousness.

Her pony-cart ferried them to cottage gardens, manors,
farmhouses, until he could imagine stone backbones—
terraces, walls, paths—for what she called *incidents,*
the ways thyme invaded steps, roses festooned
enclaves into green petal-luminous rooms.

II

Their last grand project when she was 74:
half a million bodies had never come home:
trodden over, scraped under Front Lines mud.
How to ever forget what would never return? A scheme,

then, for facsimile cemeteries abroad, and who knew
restful, leafy places best? Edwin Luytens decreed
sentinel trees: *cypresses or pyramidal oaks. The graves
will face eastward, as our men when they fell.*

Universal headstones, not crosses, he said,
of white Portland stone, 73,000 names
inscribed. She imagined walls
overgrown with privet, honeysuckle, clematis,
and around the headstones, cottage garden flowers.

She grew them herself: white thrifts,
pansies, columbine. Bright, low flowers,
so the names on headstones could be seen,
planted close together so the falling rain
would never stain the names with dirt.

SPRING

FAILED INVOCATION TO THE MUSE

Who would not seek the blessing of the Muse,
she who imparts poetic frenzy from the gods?
  Classy classic babes
  on the cover of my book...

Daughters of Apollo and Mnemosye
they each bring inspiration from the source.
  Casual tendrils escaping piled curls
  A casual breast escaping pleated robes...

The sacred muses are Euterpe, she
of flutes and lyric poetry; Clio, muse
of history; Thalia, she
of comedy and pastoral poetry;
Erato, muse of love poetry;
  Erato like Errato:
  Why do fools fall in love?

Calliope, epic poetry;
  So many plugging poetry—
  the gods know
  we need the help...

Melpomene, muse of tragedy;
Urania, astronomy; Terpsichore,—
  What a line-up—
  how many are there?

—dance; and Polyhymnia, sacred
poetry, the nine who bring divine ecstasy.
  What would you call all nine?
  Synchrony? sodality?
  —pantheon I can't quite imagine
  in my backyard.

If you would see into the minds of gods,
the muses channel from that silver stream.
    But which one to call on?
    Or could they be like back-up singers,
    a doo-wap chorus of all nine?

Summon she whose intercession you desire
that she may bring you gifts of sacred words.
    So do any of them weed?
    Shovel compost, prune or plant?

Their labors show more worthy charms;
Their feet are never sullied by the earth.
    No dirty wellies, stretched out socks?
    I hope they're not scared of worms?

Their eyes are raised to heaven's lofty heights
Not cast down to the lowest, legless things.
    Dissing worms? They're my BFF's.
    I'm questioning statuesque…

Their beauty mirrors purity of mind.
Their virtues are reflected in their dance.
    Maybe you need a cis guy
    to see the allure.
    Don't think this will work out.
    Maybe we can still be friends.

THAT BLUE

One day after the eternal winter,
the scilla gush out of the ground
in a tide that laps
at the sidewalk. Cold wind
rakes them into ripples
so they make a lake on the lawn.

This blue shimmering with violet
makes the sky seem pale.
You can find it across centuries
in beads, ribbons, velvet,

concocted on the palettes
of Gauguin and Van Gogh,
favored by the Fauves,
those *wild beasts* of art.

A blue that makes you pause
as if listening for music;
maybe you could
wish on it
for something
you'd forgotten
you wanted.

BECAUSE THE SPARROWS

*The house sparrow is not an obligate commensal of humans
as some have suggested.*

Common as pennies, they mob
the feeder, empty it in a day—
nothing left for finches, wrens,
chickadees— birds from the genus
Passeridae, meaning
flutterer.

I rush out to chase them, flapping,
absurd, a woman chasing birds
from her feeder. Their nests block
the gutters and at 4:30 a.m.
they begin what Yeats called
the brawling of a sparrow
in the eaves.

I rail against them till the day
I find one dead beneath the window,
smaller than half my palm,
bead eyes glazed, legs thin
as string, whorled feathers intricate
as Chinese ink brush landscapes.

That day I fly to tend my mother,
a misfit in my kitchen.
The impossible things she's said to me
are carved on my heart. All the ways
she tries to please seem denials
of what I love, ugly ornaments
for the Christmas tree—

until I have to change
the dressing from her surgery.
Embarrassed, she lies face
down on her sateen bedspread
while I lift the pad to see the maroon
puncture near her backbone,
incision on her softening flesh.
Only then do I see
how wrong I've been, becoming
someone to be defended from.

SPRING SNIPPINGS

TOUGH LOVE
Don't water seedlings:
they need to send thin roots deep
Forking for water

NEW
Carry a baby
to see Spring starting over
and for the first time

SEED TRAY I
Who taught seeds to do
backflips from root threads, pop up
wearing seed husk caps?

ALL YOU CAN EAT
Fifty crocus bulbs
fall-planted purple blossoms
spring bunny buffet

SEED TRAY II
Noon sun lights up fuzz
along red stems, like soft fur
above my son's lips

MORNING ON THE DECK
Crank the umbrella—
Jumbo blue morning glory
opening to sun

OUTSIDER

for Rafi and Cavi

Is it my Polish rootstock
that compels me each spring
to scrabble in frozen dirt,
rump in the air, for all to see?

As soon as I can wrench apart
barely-thawed clods, I'm shoving in
the wrinkled moons of peas
with my numb thumbs.

People may call me Crazy Lady
when they see me plodding
through snow, watering can in hand,
to tilt up the lid of my cold frame.

A slide of slush, reek of fungal earth,
and I veer in with my can, saying
to the stubby sprigs inside,
Here babies, here's your rain.

I don't remember names
of neighbors, but I remember
salvia, dahlia, polemonium.
Out all hours, all weathers—

for company a pair of neighbor boys
who whip by each spring
on a new mode of transportation:
trikes, scooters, bikes, skateboards.

When they drive cars, I'll be alone.
Inside, family are calling,
snapping on lights.
No supper yet, again.

But when I leave on spring mornings,
blue flax petals are blowing
across the driveway. And when I
straighten, late afternoons,

hands hanging heavy with dirt and tools,
I can see, snagged high in the branches
of the silver maple,
the chalky rising moon.

ACOLYTE OF GREEN

In early May I ask the kindergartners
how many greens can you see outside,
around the playground?
A thousand. Two. Sixty billion.
Seven. But I know they were busy
running and only see
the green on the alphabet rug
where we sit.

Count when you go home, I say,
with missionary zeal,
but know they won't remember.
You can never see more kinds
of green than right now.

Driving home, I think I can tell
buds have fattened
since this morning,
What kind of trees stitch
this grey-green filigree
along the highway?
And the coppery trees—
every year I forget spring trees
carry the colors of fall.

On the porch at home, seeds thrust up
from their cups on white or purple
stems wearing little caps of dirt
and husks akimbo.

I want to stay home
to watch the pale seed leaves darken,
to trace uncurling cotyledons,
taking the important inventory of greens
no one has ever seen.

HELLEBORE

Lenten rose

Every April they open like a wound—
Hellebore from the Greek: *food to punish*
pale green, plum, cream, dusty rose,—
poisonous confectionary.

She had the perfect shallow bowl for them,
nacreous shimmer like water they floated in.
I set them on the kitchen table
near the ugly ochre bottles of pills.

The trick for downward-facing blooms
is to float them in a bowl
so they turn up their centers,
corolla crown of golden nectaries,

five sepal petals splayed— an artfulness
like choreography, the June Taylor
dancers we watched Saturdays
on Jackie Gleason on TV.

That spring, in snatched moments
from the sickroom, I roamed,
found them downdrooped by hundreds
along some sun-warmed courtyard walls.

I stole them from the Horticultural Society
garden, mourning the hellebores I'd left
behind, just piercing the ground,
abandoned like my husband and son.

Kiss of eternal in the ephemeral:
Lenten roses bloom soonest, even in snow,
and last for months, stamens fusing to
a little purse of seed pods,

colors muting to papery, funereal.
When the ones I'd stolen dampened, sank,
I'd make a foray for more rose-speckled cream,
apple-green, always a bowl of beauty and sorrow.

On nearly her last foray,
my mother wandered
into the kitchen, said *These things
sure last a long time.*

PEA-PLANTING CEREMONY

Turn over the soil,
Turn over the warming soil.
All praise to worms,
loosening the earth
by spoonfuls,
pooping out pure nitrogen.

I have cast off my fleecewear
to signify winter is done.
I have taken off my turtleneck:
no longer will I be a turtle
buried in mud in a frozen pond.

Scatter, robins, you are no longer
my friends, do not hop along
behind me in search of worms
and seeds, watching me
with white-ringed eyes.

I kneel in yellow rubber boots,
and call on the old gods,
before Youtube DIY videos.

I hold pale wrinkled moons
in my palms, given over to me
by Johnny's Master Seedsmen
for cost plus postage and handling.

I bless them with my thumbs
pressing them into the earth.
Come, rain, loosen
their skins,
so dreaming white
embryos will push into light.
Come, sun,
burst them green.
Waken, now, waken, peas,
from the dark earth rise.

BIRD TALK

ARRIVALS
No, no welcome back
to you, blue-headed grackle
with black-leather strut

INVITATION
Goldfinch, don't be shy—
Fly around me sitting here:
I fill the feeders!

COMEDIAN
Zany black starling
whoop whistles in pine branches
What's so funny, hey?

JUST TO LET YOU KNOW
Returned mockingbird
sang all night in the oak tree
while you were sleeping

GANG
Squawky, arrogant
juvenile delinquent crows
cursecaw, cruise their turf

CITY BULBS

Scouting among buildings in a sharp wind
along the edges of rough weather—
where do concrete or bricks trap heat?

Knife-edge of sunlight
glint of mica in granite
and there they are

like tiny flags in a kingdom's colors
purple, golden, white:
crocuses.

They need only
once someone sunk them in earth:
parent near a playground,

student who brought some back
with groceries, a person who's since
moved or died or stays inside now.

Crammed in any patch of scrubby grass,
they'll grow even if their corms
are dug in upside down.

They've been here
all along, inevitable
buried light.

SQUIRRELY

Do you love a squirrely twirl,
admire furry highwire artists
having a whirl?
Find their tails endearingly curled?
Like how they hold their whiskety tails
aloft as they friskety hop
down the street?

Then likely you've never seen them
behead splendid tulips, leaving behind
shredded petals, green stem sticks;
or discovered maimed prize tomatoes
with incisor nips—the tiniest bites
before they're abandoned on the ground.

In spring what you see as droll antics,
amusingly frantic, are not winsome frolics,
but lustful bacchantics, not the least tantric
or romantic, just lascivious pursuits.

If only a prophylactic
stymied these prolific breeders:
If you enjoy baby squirrels,
lively and thriving,
finding them cunningly acrobatic,
you haven't found them dumpster-diving
in your squirrel-proof feeder.

Epic opposition is barely competition.
You're no match for their fiendish tactics,
so unsystematic they're nearly spastic,
around, above, beside, under,
hurling themselves is ultimately pragmatic:
they catch, they latch, and then they plunder.

PASQUEFLOWER

The common names of the Pasqueflower *Pulsatilla patens*:

Prairie anemone

Hartshorn

Blue tulip

American Pulsatilla

April Fool

Badger

Easter plant

Gosling

Wild crocus

Rock Lily

Prairie smoke

Windflower

The Dakota Indians
sang a special song
about the Pasqueflower
essentially encouraging other flowers
to follow its example
by appearing early.

THE USES OF THINGS

Matted mauve fur
of dryer lint scraped from the screen,

daughter's long hair
gleaned from a brush with a comb

thread dangling
from pants that need mending:

Mound them in a green plastic basket
that held summer berries

Find a boy otherwise
unoccupied

have him lash it with green twine
to the winter-bare crotch of a tree

Watch to see if anything with wings
will make it home.

SUMMER

YOU ASK

for Jen

what to do with your lettuce:
all bolting, going to seed.

I tell you of the English *grandes dames*
who let seeding lettuce mount
in minarets among the roses,
prizing in particular the bronze-
red frills of *Rouge d'Hiver.*

Or you could snip them an inch high,
tossing leathery leaves,
oozing bitter milk,
onto the compost heap.
Salad bowl rosettes might grow.

Or pull them out entire, fork
over the caked ground,
dig in what are called
amendments, and mix tiny
seeds with sand to sow anew.

Or maybe you,
who found time
to ask, will fall short
of time unclaimed
to follow through.

So: *Do nothing.*
Watch them shoot out
spaceman antennae
that fizz to yellow blossoms
then erupt in a frenzy
of white tufted seeds.
See if birds come forage

and strew seeds
in their droppings,
dotting the garden
with impromptu lettuce.

Most important, dear heart,
is not what's done, but only
to attend, just attend.

BUDDHA IN THE GARDEN

Buddha is where you find him.
I found mine at Pool City on Route One
near Saugus, among the birdbaths
and inflatable floatingchairs
with twin cupholders. He's the standard
concrete model with pincurls, topknot,
a Mona Lisa smile.

Brought up Catholic, I talk to him
as if he were a saint, someone who
might intervene on my behalf.
Buddha, I say, *the weeds are winning,*
overtaking the garden. What can I do?
Or *Buddha, no one sees my garden,*
the showy lilies, the new dahlias
I call Bordello Fire *and* Sunset Feathers.
The children are grown,
the grandchildren don't visit.
Should I post pictures
of my flowers on Facebook?
Do I need to get on Instagram?

Names:
In spring: Calm among Bright Blossoms Buddha
In summer: Overgrown by Bearberry Buddha
In fall: Leaf in Lap Buddha
In winter: Sno-cone Head Buddha

I circumnavigate Buddha.
No mud, no lotus, I imagine him saying
The ground under him has settled
so he leans towards me, a little askew
as I talk on my phone.
My friend is worried about her adrenals.
My grown children are seeking therapists
in the changing healthcare market.
I will listen for free,
putting them on speakerphone
so I can rip out weeds with both hands:
purslane, chickweed, twitchgrass,
hoping the neighbors won't over-
hear Trauma Drama.

I assemble little heaps of weeds
and find them days later,
small piles of brittle branched paper.

THE LAST THING

making toast this morning
still half in dreams
my mind gaped and
slipped down
a rabbit hole
to a premonition
of my death

last image
of a paper packet
with seeds inside
smaller than
pepper grains

over the years
I've learned
to tip the packet
so seeds
chute down
the crease
then I tap
the top edge
with my index finger,
firmly, gently,
so one tiny seed
at a time
hops from the lip
while the others
shake against the paper
with a mariachi whisper

this is what I will see
and hear as edges blur,
one small skill I've mastered
before the light folds in

AS WE GO

When the oaks topple like the elms,
when the ash and beech,
weakened by heat and drought,
succumb to insects or disease,
when the tall canopy is gone
and white pines and spruce
are like dead Christmas trees;
when the dirt blows away,

our children's children
can go to the Brooklyn Botanic Garden
where twelve years ago,
curators began installing
drip irrigation
to transplant a history
of postage-stamp habitats:
New Jersey pine barrens,
wetlands, kettle ponds,
limestone cliffs.

Perhaps some creatures
will make their way there—
newts, iridescent darning needles.
Perhaps our children's children
will hear the calls of birds and frogs.
They will say *oh the wind*
stirring the reeds
makes a small music.

THE FIRST TINY BUDDHA

No one believes me when I say
Tiny Buddha was stolen by squirrels.
He'll turn up, they say, but I know
he's gone. I saw the tiny peace lantern
overturned. After we'd strung
the clothesline with soda bottles
to block them from the feeders,
the squirrels were bitter:
they heard us laugh
when we saw them twirl and drop.

I imported a three-inch Buddha
to live among the elves and fairies
in the Fairy Garden I claim is for
my grandchildren. It's me
who can't resist a world writ
miniature, coleus become a Bodhi
tree, bridge with a span of inches.

Was he meant to be a missionary
to the pagan fairies? Calm
on his scallop shell he presided
until he was gone and I probed his absence
like the empty socket
of a tooth with a tongue.

THE SECOND TINY BUDDHA

A year later:
Tinkertown museum, New Mexico,
wagon wheels leaning against walls
made from 55,000 blue green brown
glass bottles cemented together
(*How To Build A Better Wall*
available for 25 cents in the gift shop.)

Green sheeny hummingbirds flitting
to ruby feeders, a mustachioed man
filming them, and I knew we'd find
another tiny Buddha here.
The iridescent hummingbirds
we see as symbols of hope
and all that's jeweled,
nearly incandescent,
were fighting fiercely, territorial,
wingbeats a kind of fury.
Life is suffering, tiny Buddha would say,
nearly inaudible.

Over the entrance, plaque emblazoned
The Best You Ever Saw.
Twenty-two rooms, tink-a-tink operetta,
handcarved miniature automated circus
and "wacky Western memorabilia,"
cheroot-smoking cowboys plonking guitars,
freak show with Fat Lady Alice from Dallas.

What's the manic melody in the juking,
jinking, jump-roping, polar bear teeter-tottering,
anvil-pounding panoply? Alfred Hitchcock
inscrutable on Boot Hill, Georgia O'Keefe,
Wonder Woman, Aunt Jemima as extras
in a waggish phantasmagoria
that sends us, staggering, soused,
to the gift shop.

Tiny Buddha was there,
with everything else we needed:
a guitar shirt, pop rocks, Chiclets box
Nativity tableau from Mexico,
rubber dinosaur head that Sadie, three,
would put on her hand, saying,
"No, Pete, don't bite my face,"
which Pete would inexplicably do, biting
her peachy cheek with his rubber teeth
while she made her squinty Popeye face.

The new tiny Buddha is the murky blue
of storm-tossed Caribbean waters
and presides now among sedums,
leptinella, miniature mondo grass,
Garden Center attempt at paradise,
so serene so far even the squirrels
haven't pillaged him.

VERGE

The extreme edge or margin; a border...The point beyond which an
action, a state, or a condition is likely to begin to occur; the brink

Wherever there is intention
to cultivate—garden
bed, patch of lawn—

the rough grasses spring up:
witchgrass, twitch, sourgrass,
crabgrass, fonio, pigeon grass:
fleshy brotherhood
that splays sideways to evade
the mower and overtake each edge.

Grasp them low
and rip them out
before they engender
a hundred thousand seeds:

They spread from any filament
of root thread left on or in
the ground. Bury the cleared edge
deep under pine needles,
salt marsh hay, cedar bark,
a smell clean
as shaving cream,—

the next day they will be there,
overgrowing the thin swords
of more orderly grass,
the planned and plotted beds.

Where have they come from
if not from a future so unlike
what we intended?

RASPBERRY INSTRUCTIONS

Leave tea steeping,
flap birds away
from the damp thicket
at the lawn's edge.

Touch each dark berry bauble:
if a gentle tug
won't free it,
leave it to sweeten
till tomorrow.

Wear long pants, long
sleeves, shoes and socks.
Never ever wade in deeper
and deeper
in your nightgown
again.

Stretching for the blackest berry,
you will drop
the fattest ones.
Bending for the low ones,
you'll let the sweetest ones,
cupped to your body,
tumble.
You will believe
you'll learn from this.

Pulled from white cone haws,
the hollow jewel domes
will fit on a child's finger
like blue black afros
or bubble hats.
They ink clothes
and fingers, wooden counters,
like blood, lipstick, wine.

Rinse them
only when you eat them.
Put them in a pretty bowl
to become
all the berries
of summer.

FIELD DAY AT SPY POND

Nobody listens in school, right?
joshes the man who came
by boat across the pond
to host the water station.
He wants the fourth-graders to listen now,
to learn phosphorus from lawn fertilizer
can make algae grow so thick
he couldn't row his boat across.

But when he says *curly pond weed,*
kids mock-fight about who has
the curliest hair. Then a female mallard
shows up for crumbs, demonstrating
what *shake a tail feather* means.
It's already time to move on, past
the willows drooping into the pond.

Someone says once willows ringed
the pond and people parked on Route 2
in spring to see the pond circled
with willow yellow.
Now kids walk past the only willows
left, bending corrugated into the water,
flinging streamers of branches, their
decayed hollows condos for critters.

At the Wildlife Station, kids get nametags:
Minnow, Coyote, Housefly,
Pond Plants, Perch, Painted Turtle...
Holding onto a circle of yellow yarn,
they crisscross each other,
to show how one thing
connects to another, giggling
and poking, but also
oddly serious as they link.

Then the leader steps in: she is algae,
one cell that quickly becomes two,
becomes dozens, becomes thousands.

The Pond Plants will die, so a child
drops his yarn, and the Minnows
will go too, the Turtle...they talk it through
until everyone has dropped their yarn
and their arms hang down.

Time to move on, but they don't,
looking at each other,
until one girl pipes up *The sun
is the only thing
that lasts.*

At the Tree Station, Mr. Ellis tells them
that even though you'll find Elm
and Chestnut Streets in most American towns,
those trees are gone now.

He points to a newly-planted Red Oak,
with a green plastic cone: A Treegator
with instructions to top up the bag once a week:
*The water will drip slowly to my roots.
Thanks! I ...will return the favor someday.*

Their job now, Mr. Ellis says, is to pass
the buckets on the ground to fill it up
in under a minute twenty-five to break
the standing record. Kids pass
buckets hand to hand, careful

not to slop. They're humming
the Jeopardy theme now, tossing
buckets back in a flurry.
Stop the clock: a minute eight,
a new record. They've broken
the record, for now soaked the Red Oak,
even if they'll never get to see
a chestnut tree, an elm.

FLORA

*It was the flower that first ushered the idea of beauty into the
world the moment, long ago, when floral attraction became an
evolutionary strategy.*
Michael Pollan
The Botany of Desire

—like the morning glory
flaunting purple parasols
among the raspberry canes.
You remember me, it confides,
*I'm not lurking under leaves
like those low-down weeds.*

You remember it, yes, and its bad habits,
strangling everything, and you move
towards it, but see the carmine star
rayed out from its center.
You pause as the streaks draw your eye
into a white chamber, to a white pistil,
white stamens delicately leaking pale pollen.

All right, just you can stay for now
you say, but look and see the bushes
are tented with clambering vines
across, among, around,
dropping seeds from papery husks.

The thicket tears to pieces
in your hands; you can't unwind
their twined grip, traversing plant
to plant to plant. Frantic, you peel,
pile, part what you can until
in despair you carry off
what fragments you can, realizing
you are dripping black seeds,
strewing them places
the vines could never reach.

PINK HIBISCUS

How did it get here?

One year
a thin stick

ejecting a jumbo pink flower
like a magician's wand.
The next year, a handful

of saucer-size blooms.
The year after,
huge bubblegum bouquet.
This July, it's tall

as a twelve-year-old, wider
than tall, cotton candy
cumulus cloud so large
I think someone is looming
at the end of the driveway.

It's begun to lean out
and accost people on the sidewalk.
No streaks, stippling, stripes
in mahogany or chartreuse
on corolla, calyx, penumbra,

just this flaunting of a childhood
nail polish color: Cameo Pink,
shameless yellow pistil
poking out
from a cloud of sunshine stamens,
dripping profligate pollen
down pink starfish lips.

Its sole mission to advertise pink,
pink of baby sunhats,
a five-year-old's tutu, Disney princesses,
announcing me to the world this way.
It doesn't know or care
I take myself more seriously.

PROVINCETOWN

saltsuck
        of ocean
tide
        uncovers
land
        stranded sand
wetted firm

                    dusk
looses
                    petals
from the roses
                    attar
of pomegranates
                    and laughter

purple scar
                    along a hip
still shiny?
                    fingers
want
                    to heal it
lips

WHAT HAPPENS

By August, the sunflowers I meant to up-
root, sprouted from last year's birdseed,
are nine feet tall, shading small

eggplants and peppers, stunting
nasturtiums to doll-sized blooms.
Summer blossoms have exploded and gone

but in fall these flowers tower
over us, lemon, mahogany, gold.
Bees drag side-bags of yellow pollen

to their furred centers, iridescent
wasps vibrate among them. A few heads
dangle limp, mandala centers

hardening to cardboard kernels,
nimbus of stiff green exclamation
marks surrounding them.

If squirrels don't come to bend
and break the stems and strip
the studded seeds, then birds

will come for them all winter— finches
and chickadees, riding
the hollow stalks like hobby horses,

grey juncos flirting white tails
and foraging what's fallen and we'll look
up and out our frost-starred windows.

SUMMER SNIPPINGS

SIDEWALK TALK
Man says his daughter
learned colors from my flowers
she saw walking by

QUESTION
Has the rain started?
or is that sound of rain drops
just leaves' susurrus?

WEIGELA OBSTACLE
How to come and go?
pink blossoms block the doorway:
stay and sit, sip tea.

IN BLOSSOMS
Tomato plants hum
tiny vibrating kazoos:
bumble bees bumbling

END OF DAY
Clipping dead roses
pale pink petals flutter down
moths in purple dusk

STANLEY'S GARDEN

for Stanley Kunitz 1905-2006

Keeping the ocean on my left,
I wended through Provincetown
the summer after he died,
past the landscape galleries,
roller skating drag queens,
the ice cream and T-shirt shops,
and hand-carried dogs
with apologetic eyes—

to a quieter part of town.
I didn't know if I could find
his house, but there
was the rusty gate.

Here were the good bones of the stone
terraces he'd built, hauling loads
of seaweed from the beach
half a century ago.

I'd thought to find it somber,
overgrown since he'd died.
But the leaves and petals
shimmied in the sunlight,
his beloved wind anemones
nearly vibrating with joy.

He'd caressed these plants,
just as, the one time
I met him and read him a poem,
he took my face gently
in his hands, a poet
a hundred years old
touching me as if
I were a flower.

ACKNOWLEDGEMENTS

Thanks to the editors of the following publications for previously publishing the following poems, sometimes in slightly different versions or with different titles. "As We Go" in Gravitas; "Spy Pond in Winter" and "Field Day at Spy Pond" were requested by the Friends of Spy Pond and first appeared in their newsletters. "Faulty" appeared in pulse; "The Last Thing" in The Boston Writing Project Newsletter; "Pink Hibiscus" in Snapdragon; "Verge" in Remembered Arts Journal and "Welcome Poem" in Random Sample. "That Blue" won second prize in the Romancing the Square/ Capitol Square project sponsored by the Mass Cultural Council. Another version of that poem, "Home/April" is on display in Boston City Hall from 2019-2020.

With deep gratitude to the many members of our Poetry Tribe who have taught me that so often generosity runs deep in what we do: Alan Shapiro, Martha Collins and Laurie Rosenthal for their diligent help with this manuscript. Ross Gay, Fred Marchant, and Marie Howe who helped guide me in discovering the possibilities of poetry. John Burt, Liza Halley, Jane Howard and Pamela Powell, who have assisted me in multitudinous ways in my role as Poet Laureate of Arlington, MA. Kyle James, Technology Angel, who miraculously manifested this book in print form.

I'm also deeply indebted to my family, husband David and children Dylan, Megan and Tristan, who forbore my many hours in the garden and penning poems. And to Jimby Anderson and True/Serious Ryndes for their hospitality in an improvised one-person writer's colony that provided the rare opportunity to revise while being dappled.

Cathie Desjardins is a lifelong literacy teacher and writer who has worked with all ages from kindergartners to seniors and graduate students. A licensed reading specialist and K-12 educator, she has also taught at UMass/Dartmouth, Suffolk University, UMass/Boston, Lesley University, and Cambridge, Boston and Arlington Adult Education centers, as well as Grub Street. Her first book of poems, *With Child*, is about pregnancy and interactions with a newborn. Her writing has been published in *The Christian Science Monitor*, *Cognoscenti* (WBUR's online magazine), YANKEE magazine and numerous newspapers, periodicals and literary journals. She was selected as Poet Laureate of Arlington, MA, for 2017-2019.